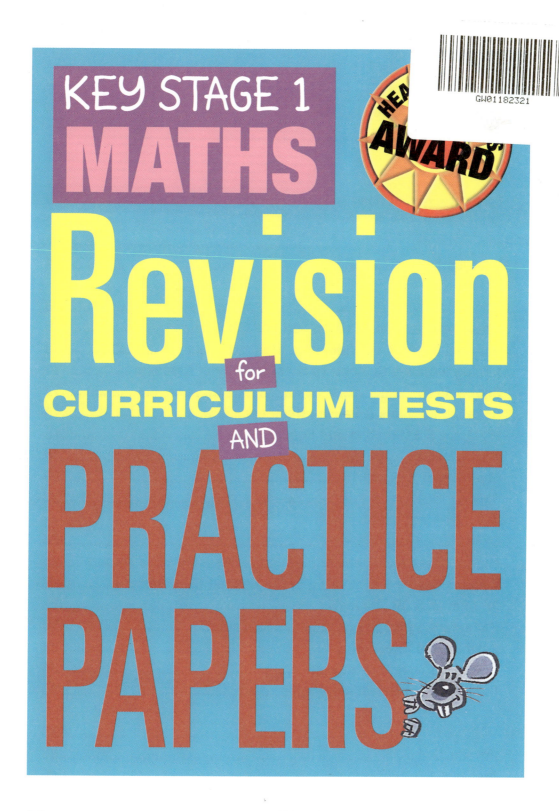

Authors
Jayne Greenwood
Holly Linklater
Susan Roberts

Consultant Editor
John Cattermole

This is a Flame Tree Book
First published in 2002

02 03 04 05

10 9 8 7 6 5 4 3 2 1

ISBN 1-903817-65-X

Flame Tree is part of
The Foundry Creative Media Company Ltd
Crabtree Hall, Crabtree Lane, Fulham,
London SW6 6TY

Visit the Foundry website: www.foundry.co.uk/flametree

Copyright © The Foundry 2002

Thanks to Dave Jones for the technical illustrations.

Thanks also to Vicky Garrard, Julia Rolf, Colin Rudderham, Graham Stride, Nick Wells and Polly Willis.

All rights reserved. No part of this publication may be reproduced, stored in a retrieval system, or transmitted in any form or by any means, electronic, mechanical, photocopying, recording or otherwise, without the prior permission of the publisher.

A copy of the CIP data for
this book is available from the British Library.

Printed in Croatia

Contents

Foreword: Aim of Head Teacher's Award Series 3

REVISION SECTION 4
Introduction 4

Number and Algebra 6
Whole Numbers Up to 100 & Odd and Even Numbers 6
Hundred Squares and Adding to 100 8
Adding Numbers to Make 10 & Adding Bigger Numbers 10
Subtraction 12
Doubling Numbers & Halving Numbers 14
Fractions & Estimating and Rounding 16
Multiplication 18
Multiples of 2, 5 and 10 20
Solving Problems & Puzzles 22

Shape, Space and Measure 24
Length, Mass and Capacity & Estimate, Measure and Compare 24
Reading Scales & Measuring to the Nearest Centimetre 26
2D Shapes & 3D Shapes 28
Patterns & Symmetry 30
Position and Direction 32
Telling the Time & Money 34
Data Handling & Reading Graphs 36

PRACTICE PAPERS 38
Introduction 38
Oral Test 1 40
Test 1 42
Oral Test 2 58
Test 2 60

Answers: Tests 1 & 2 76
Answers: Revision Section Questions 80

2

Foreword

In today's ever-changing educational climate in which targets, levels of achievement and school league-tables grab headline news, it is important to remember what is at the core of it all: the education of your child.

Children learn at different speeds and achieve different levels during their early years at school, so it is important that a child is encouraged to work to the best of his or her ability, whatever their standard.

The Head Teacher Awards, which many schools use, is a simple, yet highly effective way to motivate children. In the classroom a child may be given an HTA for a particularly good piece of work, or for trying hard in a subject they may struggle with, or for neat handwriting, fluent reading, or imaginative creative writing. The list is endless, yet the effect of the HTA on the child is great: they feel valued and that something they have really tried hard at has been noticed.

The idea behind the Head Teacher's Award Series is much the same as the award-scheme practised in the classroom. This book has been devised for use by children who are coming up to their National Tests at the end of Key Stage One. Not only does it reinforce all the information they need to know for their Tests through a series of fun and practical questions and activities, it gives children a chance to work a little harder and be rewarded with a Head Teacher's Award. Throughout the book, one or two questions on each page have a HTA symbol next to them, indicating that that particular question or activity may require a little more work or a more lateral approach in order to get the answer right. It is up to the parent to decide what the award should be (we are not advocating bribery here!), something to make the child feel they have reached a target. It may be that you decide with your child that they have to get a certain number of HTAs in the book before they can have their 'award', based on their ability.

Written by teachers of Key Stage One children, the aim of this book is that through a combination of revision, motivational aids and practical tests that the child can take in a familiar and comfortable environment, they will be as prepared as they can be for the National Tests that they will take at the end of Key Stage One.

John Foster
Former Head Teacher of St Marks Junior School, Salisbury.

Introduction

What are SATs?

The Standard Attainment Tests, or SATs (also known as National Curriculum Tests, or NCTs) are a government initiative that have been in place for several years. They are designed to give an indication of the level at which your child is working at the end of each Key Stage. Children who are in Years 1 and 2 study Key Stage 1 of the National Curriculum. At the end of Year 2, in May, the children are tested on their knowledge and skills in two core subjects, maths and English.

How This Book Works

In most schools, maths is taught through the daily numeracy lesson, which covers and regularly revisits all aspects of the maths curriculum. In school, most mathematical concepts will have been taught through practical situations, with children having first-hand experiences. For example, money is taught through the setting up of a class shop, with children buying and selling goods and handling money. There is an emphasis on mental calculations within the numeracy curriculum and your child will be encouraged to use a variety of methods and strategies to find answers and to explain the process they used.

Revision Section

This guide has been designed to help your child revise the curriculum and prepare for the SAT. Remember – this is a revision aid and if your child is not confident in a particular area then it is possible that the aspect of that topic has yet to be covered at school. The revision aspects of this guide closely follow the curriculum, methods and language that most schools use. Try to keep to these guidelines to avoid confusing your child.

Topics can be covered in any order and it is suggested that little and often is the best approach. It is important to work together on these tasks at a time when your child is fresh, keen and best able to concentrate. The end of the day is not always a good time to work on revision, as your child will no doubt have worked hard at school and will not be enthusiastic about more work! Each double-page spread has been designed to cover a unit that would be a realistic amount for your child to cover in one sitting.

Questions

Each of these units covers the key objectives for each area of the curriculum, with a clear explanation of the topic. The questions are designed to encourage your child to investigate the topic outlined on the page. The activities provide an opportunity for your child to consolidate his or her learning in a fun way.

Parent's Guides

The parent's guides offer further explanations of the key objectives and the vocabulary used in the book, as well as offering advice on how to help your child approach these tasks.

Head Teacher's Awards

On each double page you will notice the Head Teacher's Award symbol. This award has been designed to provide motivation and acknowledge success. Your child will need your help to establish whether or not they have successfully answered the question, and this in turn will help you to gauge their level of understanding and how you might be able to support their learning in the future.

Practice Papers

When your child has confidently covered the revision section at the beginning of this book, there is a series of practice questions for them to work through that are similar to those that they will face in the real tests. Further details about these questions can be found on pages 38 and 39.

What You Can Do to Help

It is important that your child does not feel pressurised by these activities as they are designed to be interesting and enjoyable. Remember, this is not new learning, but sets of activities which consolidate established learning. You can support your child by providing practical equipment such as buttons for counters. This will enable your child to visualise the concepts being taught and extend their learning beyond the activities suggested.

Motivate your child to succeed. Reward your child for every Head Teacher's Award they get – discuss this with your child to agree a suitable reward.

Keep the tests in perspective. Remember that SATs are as much a test of the school's success as of your child's ability, so do not cause your child anxiety by over-stressing the importance of the exams. Nor are SATs an end in themselves; they are part of a whole process designed to ensure that your child has a solid foundation for later learning and success.

Number and Algebra

Count, Read and Order Whole Numbers Up to 100

Counting On and Back

Activities

1. Pointing carefully to each number, can you count along the mouse's tail starting at 0 and ending at 100?

2. Place the point of a pencil somewhere along the mouse's tail. Starting at this point, can you count to 100 and count back to 0?

Questions

1. What number do you get if you count on 7 from 54?
2. What number do you get if you count back 5 from 63?
3. Count on from 46 to 51. How many did you count?
4. Count back from 93 to 88. How many did you count?
5. Can you count along the mouse's tail in units of 2, 3, 4 and 5?

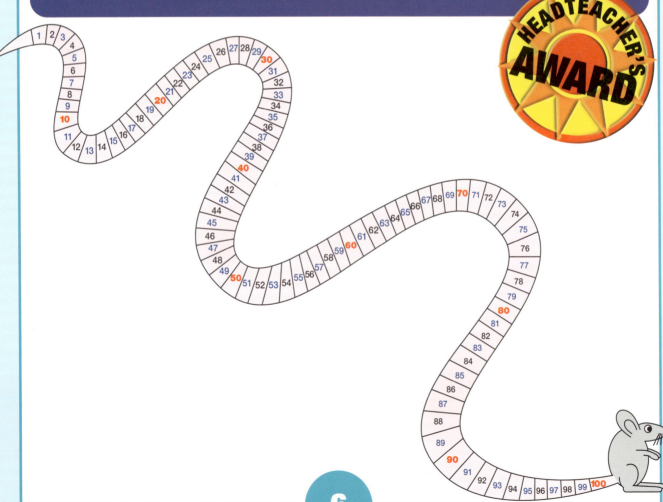

Number and Algebra

Odd and Even Numbers

Activity

Start at 0 and count in 2s along the mouse's tail. Start at 1 and count in 2s along the mouse's tail. What do you notice?

Questions

1. Take a handful of counters, count how many there are. Is this an odd or even number? Divide the counters into equal piles to find out.

2. Which numbers would come next in these sequences?
6, 8, 10, 12,   ?
43, 45, 47,   ?
64, 66, 68,   ?

3. Which number is missing from this sequence?
83, ?, 87, 89

Remember

It is a good idea to keep practising counting on and back: start at a 2-digit number and count on in 1s to 100 or back to 0. Don't count the number that you start on!

Parent's Guide

Count, read and order whole numbers up to 100: Your child needs to be able to count on and back along the number line, recognising and saying all the numbers. Practising with you first will help them to complete the activities on this page.

Odd and even numbers: The odd and even numbers can be identified by the different-coloured numbers. Help your child to understand that an even number divides exactly by 2, and that when an odd number is divided by 2 there is 1 left over.

Number and Algebra

Hundred Squares and Adding to 100

Using a Hundred Square

Hundred squares are useful when ordering numbers. When numbers in the times table are coloured in, there is a pattern which shows you which number comes next.

Move across add one

1	2	3	4	5	6	7	8	9	10
11	12	13	14	15	16	17	18	19	20
21	22	23	24	25	26	27	28	29	30
31	32	33	34	35	36	37	38	39	40
41	42	43	44	45	46	47	48	49	50
51	52	53	54	55	56	57	58	59	60
61	62	63	64	65	66	67	68	69	70
71	72	73	74	75	76	77	78	79	80
81	82	83	84	85	86	87	88	89	90
91	92	93	94	95	96	97	98	99	100

Move down add ten

Parent's Guide

To become familiar with a hundred square your child needs to understand that moving across is adding 1 and moving down is adding 10. Encourage your child to recognise the patterns involved with multiples of 2 and 10.

Ask questions such as:
What is 1 more/less than ;?
What is 10 more/less than ;?

Number and Algebra

Questions

1. What do you notice about the way the numbers are ordered on the hundred square?

2. Which numbers are in the 10 times table?

3. Which numbers are in the 2 times table?

Activity

This is a part of a hundred square. Try to fill in the missing numbers.

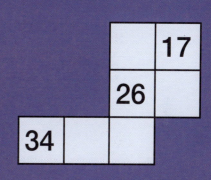

Number and Algebra

Adding Numbers to Make 10

This sign ✚ means to add up or addition.

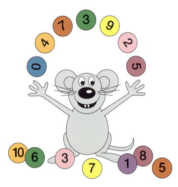

Adding Up

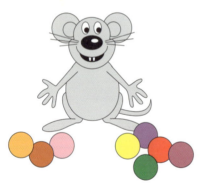

3 + 5 = 8

You can add numbers up in any order. If you swap over the numbers you are adding you will get the same answers. Try it and see!

5 + 3 = 8

Questions

1. Do you know all the ways to make 10 by adding two numbers?

2. How quickly can you say all the pairs of numbers that make 10?

Activities

1. Choose one of the numbers on a ball that mouse is juggling. How much would you have to add to that number to make 10?

2. Find that missing number by looking at the balls on the floor and matching it with its partner.

Number and Algebra

Adding Bigger Numbers

When you add two bigger numbers it is a good idea to make the sum **easier** for yourself! You can do this by making one of the numbers 10, as it is easy to add numbers on to 10.

EXAMPLE:
To add 9 and 5 together, make 10 by taking 1 away from the 5 and putting it with the 9 to make 10. You will then have 10 and 4 which makes 14.

Activity

Can you add up the number of objects in each of the groups above?

Questions

1. Estimate which group has the largest number of objects and count that first. Now count the smaller group. Can you make the larger group up to 10 by taking some from the smaller group?

2. Now add the smaller number on to the larger number.

Parent's Guide

Number bonds to 10: If your child can learn by heart all the ways to make 10, so that they have quick recall of them, this will really help them with mental maths in many situations.

For example, show them or tell them a number, e.g. 6, and get them to show or say to you the number that needs to be added to it to make 10.

Help your child to add two numbers by encouraging them to look for a way to make 10. This is called bridging through 10 and is a useful strategy to learn.

Number and Algebra

Subtraction Stories: Tales of Taking Away

The sign — means to take away or subtract.

If you have a plate of 8 sandwiches, and 4 of them are taken away, you would have 4 left.

take away

equals

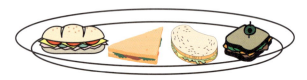

8 − 4 = 4

Remember
Always put the biggest number first.

Activities

Draw your own pictures of plates of party food to help you answer these questions.

1. 10 − 3 = ?

2. 12 − ? = 10

3. ? − 3 = 6

Questions

Now try and answer these questions. Use counters to help you.

1. 4 − 2 = ?

2. ? − 6 = 2

3. ? − ? = 4

4. Four minus two equals?

5. Subtract six from ten

Number and Algebra

Subtraction, or **taking away**, is the opposite to **adding**.

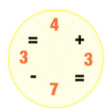

There were 4 pencils on the floor.

Martha dropped 3 more.

4 + 3 = 7

Meetali picked up 3 pencils.

7 − 3 = 4

Questions

1. Can you re-tell this story using counters?

2. Did you end up with the same number of counters that you started with?

Activity

Can you make up some number stories about adding and taking away using these numbers? You might want to use some of the words below in your story.

3, 6, 9
2, 4, 6
10, 1, 9

take away
subtract
how many are left
how much less is … than …

Parent's Guide

Here is a list of Key Stage One vocabulary for add or subtract which your child should be familiar with:

add (+)
  – together
  – total
  – plus
  – sum

subtract (−)
  – minus
  – take away
  – difference
  – how much more is; than

Encourage your child to respond to oral or written questions phrased in a variety of ways using numbers 0 to 20.

It will help your child if they can learn to visualise the sum, for example by thinking of it as a practical problem.

Number and Algebra

Doubling Numbers

If these 4 shoes had their partners you would have doubled the number to 8.

Double 5 is 10

....

....

....

....

Question
Can you work out what the numbers of these groups of shoes would be if they were doubled? The first one is done for you.

Activity
Learn your 2 times table by heart – this will really help you with doubling numbers.

Number and Algebra

Halving Numbers

When you **halve** a number you **divide** it into 2 or **share it out** between 2 people.

If you took away one shoe from each pair of these shoes you would have **halved** the number.

Half of 6 is 3

Questions

1. Can you count how many individual shoes there are in each group in the boxes below?

2. Now can you work out what half of that number would be? The first one has been done for you.

Activities

Can you solve these problems?

1. There are 10 eyes looking out of a mouse hole. How many mice are there?

2. Mica found 16 black gloves in a box. How many pairs do they make?

HEADTEACHER'S AWARD

Parent's Guide

If your child can learn by heart all the doubles of numbers to 10, this will really help with mental calculations. Learning the 2 times table is an excellent way to do this.

Halving is the inverse of doubling and quick recall of this will also help with mental maths. Play dividing or sharing-out games with sweets or counters to reinforce this.

Number and Algebra

Fractions

Look at these pictures of cheeses. When a whole cheese is divided into 2 parts, each part is one half ($\frac{1}{2}$).

1 whole cheese

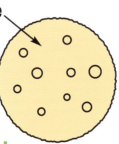
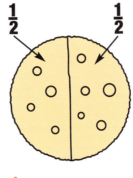
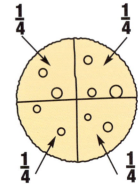

When the cheese is divided into 4 equal parts, each part is one quarter ($\frac{1}{4}$).

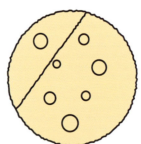
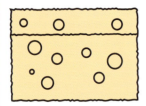

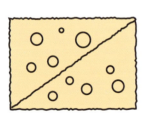
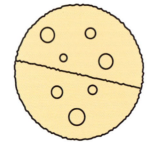

Questions

1. Which cheeses are not divided in half?

2. How many quarters are there in one half?

3. How many quarters are there in 2 whole cheeses?

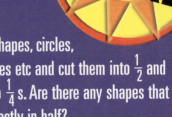

Activity

Draw some 2D shapes, circles, squares, rectangles etc and cut them into $\frac{1}{2}$ and then $\frac{1}{2}$ again into $\frac{1}{4}$s. Are there any shapes that cannot be cut exactly in half?

Parent's Guide

Reinforce fractions through cutting cakes and chocolate into equal parts to represent $\frac{1}{2}$ and $\frac{1}{4}$. Discuss with your child which foods are more difficult to cut exactly into $\frac{1}{2}$, such as those with irregular shapes.

Number and Algebra

Estimating and Rounding

To **estimate** is to make a sensible guess. When you estimate a number of objects you **do not count them**.

To **round** is to move the number to the **nearest 10**. It only moves up to the next 10 if it is half way or more. For example, 44 is closer to 40 than it is to 50 but 46 is closer to 50 than it is to 40. If the number ends in 5, e.g. 55, we round it up to the **nearest 10**, e.g. 60.

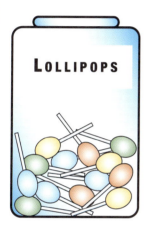
LOLLIPOPS

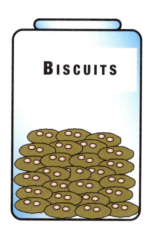
BISCUITS

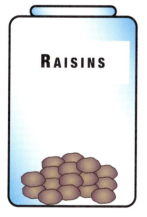
RAISINS

NUTS

Questions

1. Can you estimate which jars have less than 20 objects in them?

2. Can you count the objects in each jar and round them to the nearest 10?

Activity

Put different amounts of marbles or sweets in a jar. First estimate how many you have, then count them and round them to the nearest 10.

Parent's Guide

It is important that your child understands that an estimate is an accurate guess and not necessarily the correct answer. When rounding, your child will need to understand where half way between two multiples of 10 is. You could practise this by choosing numbers and finding them on a number line to help visualise where they lie between two multiples of 10.

Number and Algebra

Multiplication

The sign x means **multiply** or **lots of**.

Look at Mouse's family gathering below, and at some of the things they had to eat and drink. Then try and answer the questions on the next page.

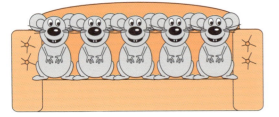
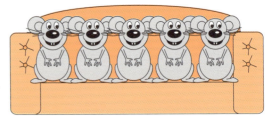
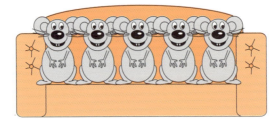

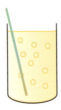

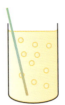
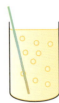

Number and Algebra

Questions

1. There are 3 cakes and 3 candles on each cake. How many candles are there altogether?

   3 + 3 + 3 is the same as 3 x 3 which equals ....

2. There are 6 special biscuits. Each biscuit has 2 sweets on top. How many sweets are there altogether?

   6 x 2 = ...

3. There are 5 glasses of lemonade with 10 bubbles in each glass. How many bubbles are there altogether?

   5 x 10 = ...

Activities

Now test yourself with these questions!

1. 3 lots of 5 = ...

2. 9 x 2 = ...

3. 10 groups of 7 totals ....

4. 2 + 2 + 2 = ...

5. 2 x 10 = ...

6. Can you work out how many flags there are on the bunting without counting them all? There are the same number of flags for each colour. ....

Parent's Guide

Help your child to understand that the multiplication sign (x) means 'groups of' or 'lots of', which is the same as repeated addition.

If your child can count confidently in 2s, 5s and 10s, this will help them with multiplication.

Number and Algebra

Multiples of 2, 5 and 10

The 2 Times Table

1 x 2 = 2
or 1 lot of 2 is 2

Tip
Practice saying your 2 times table over and over again until you can say it really fast.

The 5 Times Table

1 x 5 = 5
or 1 lot of 5 petals is 5

9 x 5 = 45
or 9 lots of 5 petals is 45

The 10 Times Table

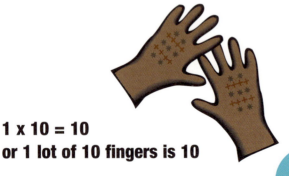

1 x 10 = 10
or 1 lot of 10 fingers is 10

Questions (2 x table)

1. How well do you know your 2 times table?

2. Can you say it in under 1 minute?

Activity

Use counters or pennies and carry on setting out pairs to show the 2 times table.

Activity (5 x table)

Ask an adult to help you to use paint to print rows of 5 objects on to a large sheet of paper. You could print your finger-tips or cut out a shape from a potato.

Questions (10 x table)

1. Can you use your fingers to count in 10s to 100?

2. Are you able to say the 10 times table as '1 10 is 10, 2 10s are 20' etc.?

Activities

Set up a play shop where everything costs 10p. You could use your toys or books. Take turns with a friend to buy and sell.

1. How quickly can you add up the bill?

2. Can you work out how much it will be if you buy more than 10 items?

Number and Algebra

Practise What You Have Learned!

Question

Can you say the multiplication that each group of pictures is showing?

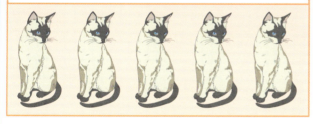

Parent's Guide

It is important that your child recognises the multiplication sign and understands what it means. Children need to know by heart the multiplication facts for the 2, 5 and 10 times tables. A good starting point is to learn to count in that number before moving on to learn it as a times table.

Number and Algebra

Solving Problems

These are the **signs** that tell you what you have to do **to sort out a problem**.

Remember
The sign ÷ means to divide, or to share.

Questions

Can you say which sign you would like to use to solve these problems?

1. Mr Samuel deals 3 cards to himself and 3 to each of his friends. How many cards are there altogether?

....

2. Mouse puts 11 toy soldiers in rows but knocks over 3. How many are now standing?

....

3. Mouse throws a pair of dice. One lands on 6 and the other on 4. What do they make altogether?

....

4. Mouse has 20 marbles. He shares them equally between himself and a friend. How many do they each have?

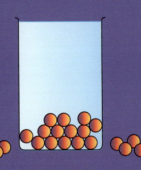

....

Activity

Make up a word story like the ones about Mouse above for each of these questions:

4 + 6 = 10
11 − 5 = 6
3 × 4 = 12
10 ÷ 2 = 5

22

Number and Algebra

Puzzles

When solving puzzles always look carefully at **simple patterns**, or the relationship between numbers.

EXAMPLE:
Look at the numbers 2, 4, 6 – you can see that each number is two more than the one before it.

Remember
Questions that have + and x in them will have bigger numbers in the answer than appear in the question. Questions which have − and ÷ will have smaller numbers in the answer.

Question

Can you work out a pattern to find the missing numbers on these three rows of playing cards?

| 3 | 5 | 7 | ? | 11 | ? | ? | 17 |

| ? | 16 | ? | 12 | 10 | ? | 6 | ? |

| 4 | 7 | 10 | ? | 16 | ? | ? | 25 |

Activity

Here are some puzzles to try and solve:

1. Rearrange these digits so the sum of each row and column is the same.

3	3	3	...
4	4	4	...
5	5	5	...

2. Put numbers 1 to 6 in the circles so that each side of the triangle adds up to 9.

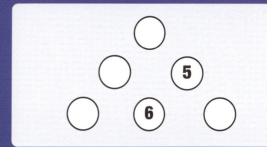

Parent's Guide
When answering puzzles, encourage your child to talk through why he or she has decided on a particular outcome and to try another method if they have been unsuccessful.

Shape, Space and Measure

Length, Mass and Capacity

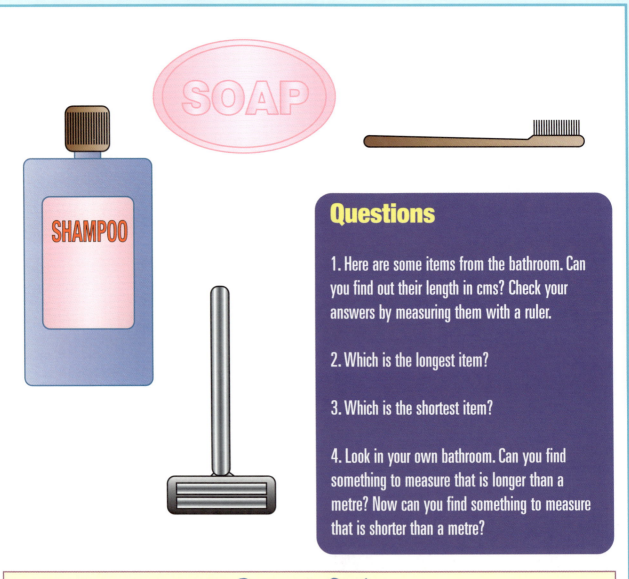

Questions

1. Here are some items from the bathroom. Can you find out their length in cms? Check your answers by measuring them with a ruler.

2. Which is the longest item?

3. Which is the shortest item?

4. Look in your own bathroom. Can you find something to measure that is longer than a metre? Now can you find something to measure that is shorter than a metre?

Parent's Guide

This page helps your child investigate length and measuring. The activities below will help your child understand capacity and weight.

Look at different bottles of shampoo and bubble bath in your bathroom. How much liquid was in them when they were bought? Find some empty bottles to experiment with when in the bath.

Weigh yourself on some bathroom scales. How much do you weigh in kgs? Can you find someone who is heavier than you? Can you find someone who is lighter than you? How much do they weigh?

Shape, Space and Measure

Estimate, Measure and Compare

Tip
An estimate is a thought-about guess. Being able to estimate is very helpful, especially when you need to check your answers.

Activities

Without counting, estimate how many of these objects there are:

1. Ducks

2. Bottles of shampoo

3. Toothbrushes

You can check your answers by counting carefully.

Parent's Guide
Encourage your child to estimate, and talk about what would be a good estimate. Discuss with your child whether it looks like there are more than 10 or less than 10, more than 5 or less than 5.

25

Shape, Space and Measure

Reading Scales

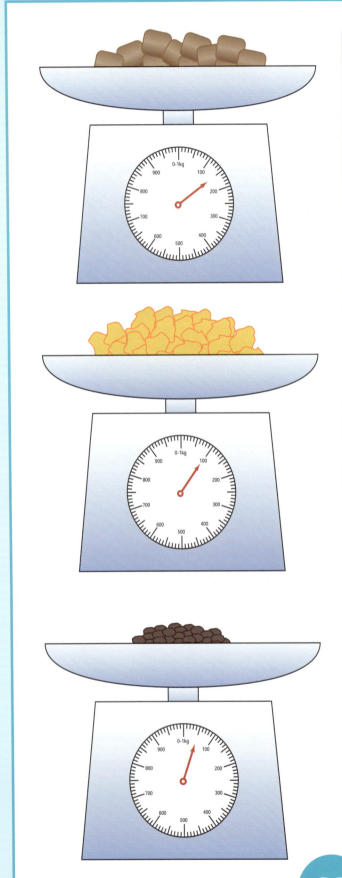

Questions

Mouse is making some cornflake cakes. Look at the scales that he is using. What are the weights of the:

1. Chocolate? ....g

2. Cornflakes? ....g

3. Raisins? ....g

4. How many grams are there in a kilogram? ....g

Activity

Using a set of kitchen weighing scales, weigh out the same quantities of chocolate, cornflakes and raisins as Mouse has done.

Get an adult to help you melt the chocolate.

Mix in the dry ingredients.

Put a tablespoon of the mixture into paper cases.

Eat when cold!

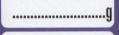

Shape, Space and Measure

Measuring to the Nearest Centimetre

Using a centimetre ruler, measure the lengths of each of the mice tails. What do they measure, to the nearest centimetre?

Blue ....

Red ....

Green ....

Yellow ....

Orange ....

Activity

Look in your pencil case and measure your pencil, pen, rubber, sharpener and any other small objects.

Parent's Guide

Children love to help out in the kitchen. Ask your child to weigh out ingredients for you. Look carefully at the markers on your scales and discuss how they are set out.

Using a tape measure or a ruler, measure different objects around the room. Encourage your child to read to the nearest centimetre.

Shape, Space and Measure

2D Shapes

CIRCLE
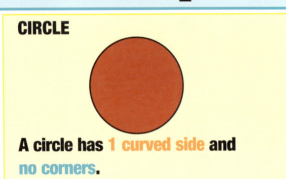
A circle has **1 curved side** and **no corners**.

TRIANGLE
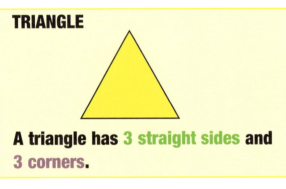
A triangle has **3 straight sides** and **3 corners**.

SQUARE
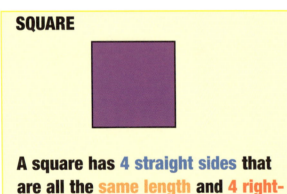
A square has **4 straight sides** that are all the **same length** and **4 right-angled corners**.

RECTANGLE
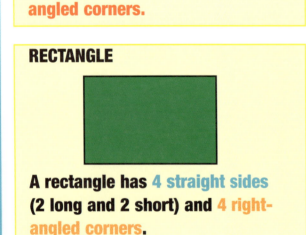
A rectangle has **4 straight sides** (2 long and 2 short) and **4 right-angled corners**.

HEXAGON
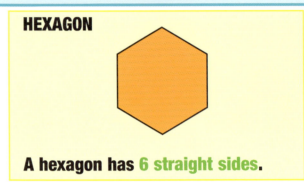
A hexagon has **6 straight sides**.

PENTAGON
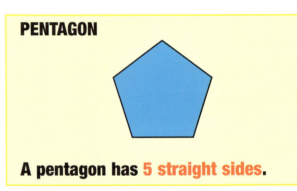
A pentagon has **5 straight sides**.

Questions

1. Can you cover over the labels next to the shapes and still name them?

2. Can you say one of the properties of each shape (e.g. a square has 4 straight sides that are all the same length)?

Activity

Draw a picture using as many of the above shapes as you can.

Colour each shape a different colour.

How many times have you used each shape?

Shape, Space and Measure

3D Shapes

CUBE

A cube has 6 faces that are all squares.

SPHERE

A sphere has 1 curved face.

CONE

A cone has 1 circular flat face and 1 curved face.

CYLINDER

A cylinder has 2 flat circular faces and 1 curved face.

CUBOID

A cuboid has 4 larger rectangular sides and 2 smaller sides that can be squares or rectangles.

TRIANGULAR PRISM

A triangular prism has 3 sides that are rectangular and 2 sides that are triangles.

Questions

1. Can you find tins, packets and boxes in your kitchen cupboards to match the shapes shown above?

2. Are you able to say the names of the shapes as you find them?

Activity

Make a collection of empty packets and containers to help you with these activities.

Use the packets to play a sorting game. Make labels of the 3D shapes you have collected and sort the boxes and containers into the correct pile.

When you have finished sorting, use the boxes to make models.

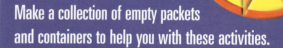

Remember
2D shapes are flat, 3D shapes are solid.

Parent's Guide

2D shapes: Use everyday situations to reinforce your child's understanding of the properties of 2D shapes. Draw round objects to see what 2D shapes you get, e.g. a circle from a round plate.

3D shapes: Children need to have a lot of experience of handling solid shapes so that they can feel the faces and understand about the properties. Letting them handle objects from your kitchen cupboards is a good way to provide this experience. Encourage your child to explore which shapes will roll or slide. You could use a pillow-case as a bag and put the containers into it, taking turns to identify shapes.

Shape, Space and Measure

Patterns

Question

Can you copy and then continue the patterns on the wallpaper in Mouse's house?

Activities

1. Look around your house and see if you can find examples of repeating patterns.

2. Now see if you can find an example of a pattern that rotates the image.

Shape, Space and Measure

Symmetry

The line that divides a shape into 2 **identical halves** is called a **line of symmetry**. Many shapes and patterns have more than one line of symmetry.

Tip
If you want to check the lines of symmetry on a pattern or picture, use a mirror.

Questions

1. Can you identify the lines of symmetry for the pictures on the lampshades?

2. One of the pictures does not have a line of symmetry; can you tell which one?

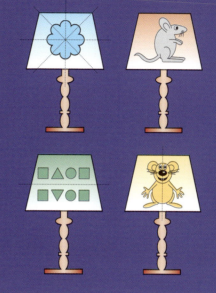

Activity

Using counters or buttons, copy these patterns onto a piece of paper. Then complete the patterns by making the other half.

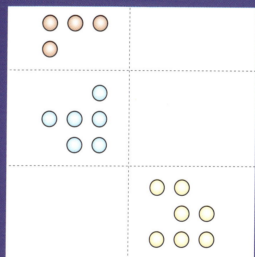

Parent's Guide

Encourage your child to look carefully at the patterns and recognise where they repeat themselves.

Help your child to recognise that a square and a rectangle have right angles at each corner. A right angle is a quarter turn. Your child needs be able to recognise patterns that have moved through a quarter and a half turn.

Shape, Space and Measure

Position and Direction

Position is the **exact location** of an object.   **Direction** is telling you **how to find it**.

These are some useful words you can use when you are describing the position and direction of something.

bottom left
bottom right
top left
top right
centre

next to
on the edge of
further away from
on top of
behind

32

Shape, Space and Measure

Question

Can you give the position of the objects in the garden (for example, the apple tree is next to the pear tree)? Use the words in the box on page 32 to help you.

Activity

Give directions for the purple mouse to go to the shed where the blue mouse is. Use directions such as one/two/three squares to the left/right/up/down. Look at where the arrows are pointing on the drawing below to help you. Make up some more yourself using different mice.

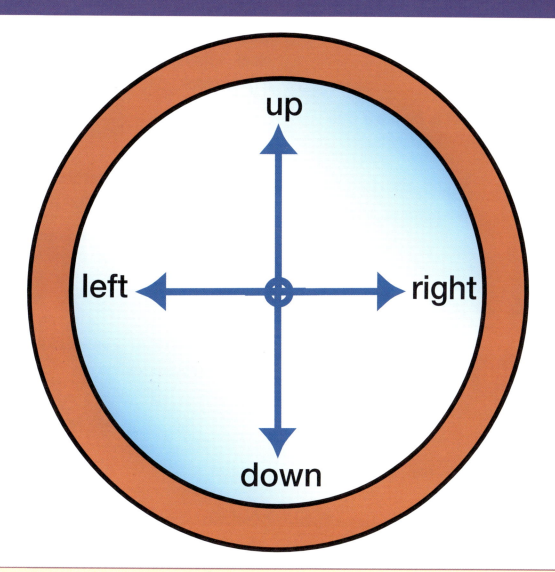

Parent's Guide

Children need to read, understand and use the vocabulary of position, movement and direction. Encourage your child to use specific vocabulary to describe where objects are in relation to one another, or to give directions on a simple grid.

Shape, Space and Measure

Telling the Time

Analogue Clocks

When the big hand is at the 12 it is always o'clock. The small hand tells you which hour it is.

When the big hand is on the 6 it is always half past the hour.

When the big hand is on the 3 it is always quarter past the hour.

When the big hand is on the 9 it is always quarter to the hour.

Question

Can you read quarter to and quarter past on both an analogue and a digital clock?

Digital Clocks

When it is an o'clock time on Mouse's clock, this is what it looks like on a digital clock.

03.00

When it is a half past time on Mouse's clock, this is what it looks like on a digital clock.

03.30

When it is a quarter past time on Mouse's clock, this is what it looks like on a digital clock.

04.15

When it is a quarter to time on Mouse's clock, this is what it looks like on a digital clock.

02.45

Parent's Guide

Talk about the job that each hand does on the clock. Help your child to understand how long a minute is, or how long five minutes is. Use everyday situations to reinforce this, e.g. can you tidy your toys away in one minute? Reinforce o'clock and half past by pointing out these times as they occur in your routine, e.g. It is your bedtime at 7 o'clock.

Your child needs to be able to read o'clock, half past, quarter to and quarter past on a 12-hour digital clock, they do not need to understand the 24-hour clock at this stage.

Shape, Space and Measure

Money

Tom and Harriet each have a money box. Look carefully at the coins that are in each box and then answer the questions below.

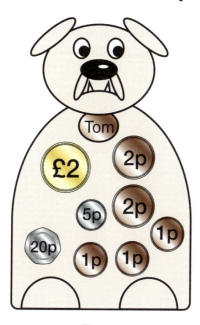

Tom

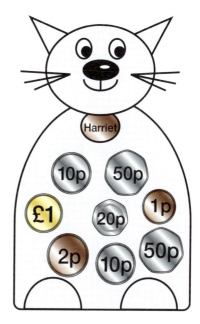

Harriet

Questions

1. Harriet buys a paintbrush which costs 51p. Which coins should she use to pay for it?

2. Tom wants to buy some sweets. Which 3 coins should he use to buy the most sweets? Which 3 coins should he use to buy the least?

3. Harriet bought 2 ice lollies at 35p each. She paid using her £1 coin. How much change did she get? Which coins might she have been given?

Activities

1. Work out how much money Harriet has in her money box.

2. Work out how much money Tom has in his money box.

3. Can you tell who has the most money?

Parent's Guide

Check that your child is able to recognise all the coins, and understands their relative value. Encourage your child to explain how he or she worked out the answers for the questions. If possible, re-enact the story with real money.

Shape, Space and Measure

Data Handling – Reading Graphs

Here is a bar chart showing the birthdays of Mouse's family.

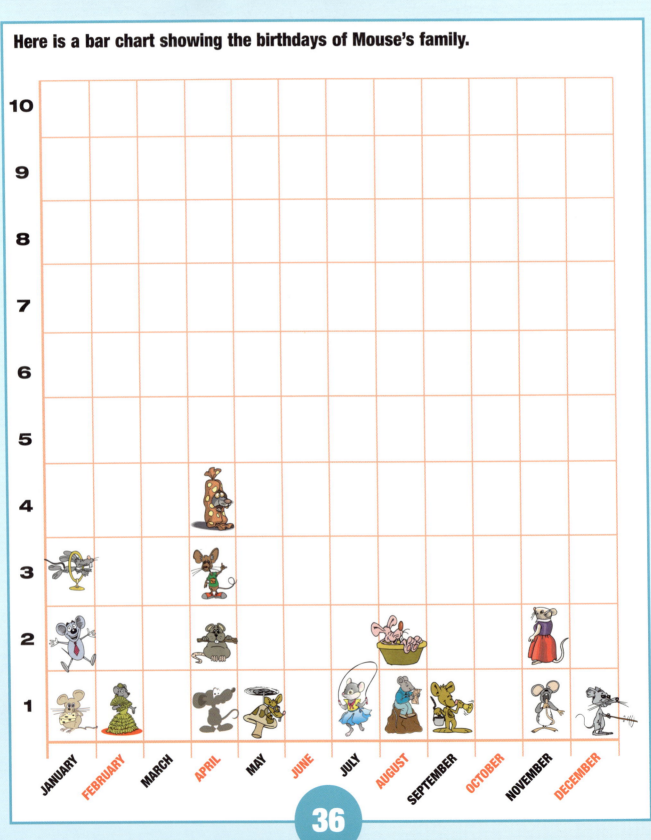

36

Shape, Space and Measure

Questions

1. How many mice have their birthdays in April?

2. Which months have two mouse birthdays?

3. How many mice have birthdays in March?

4. Which month has the largest number of birthdays?

5. How many mice have their birthdays in November?

6. Can you learn the order of the months of the year?

Activities

1. Make a bar chart to find out the favourite day of the week. Use squared paper to help you and set it out like the graph shown on the page opposite, with the numbers up the side and the days of the week along the bottom.

2. The days of the week are shown below to help you to spell the names. They are mixed up. Can you put them in the correct order?

3. Ask a friend or member of your family their favourite day. Colour in one square to represent that day. Use one colour crayon for one day e.g. blue for Monday, red for Tuesday etc.

4. When you have finished your chart, can you work out which is the most popular day of the week?

Tuesday Sunday Wednesday FRIDAY Monday Saturday Thursday

Parent's Guide

Your child needs to know that bar charts or graphs are ways in which we can show information. They also need to know how to read them or interpret the information. Making your own chart is an excellent way to understand the process of collecting and presenting data.

The activities described also help to reinforce aspects of time, the months of the year and days of the week. Explain to your child how the units of time are broken down and the names they have (days, weeks, months). Help your child to learn the order of the days and months; there are many simple songs and rhymes to help with this.

Practice Papers

Introduction to Practice Test Papers

The National Tests

The national testing of children at the end of Key Stage 1 (Year 2) takes place annually in May. The class teacher will have selected a date, by which point the children will have been prepared for the test. The teacher will have ensured that as far as possible normal classroom practice remains undisturbed. Your child may not be aware that anything out of the ordinary is taking place.

There is no time limit for the test; however it usually takes place on one day with a break after about 30 minutes. Discretion will be used to ensure that your child is given time to finish all the oral and written questions that they are able to do.

Some resources will usually be provided to help your child complete the test paper. These vary from year to year but usually include a centimetre ruler and some sort of structured counting apparatus such as small cubes. In order to ensure that the test is administered fairly, changes to the usual classroom layout may have been necessary so that children can work undisturbed, individually and without access to materials that could give them an unfair advantage, such as hundred squares and number lines. Children will not be allowed to discuss questions or copy answers, but they may be helped to read the question as it is written in the test booklet.

Your child will be encouraged to work through the booklet, answering as many questions as they are able and then to check their answers on completion.

Practice Papers

How are National Tests marked?

At Key Stage 1 the class teacher marks the tests. The results are reported to you as a level with a grade. The expected level for Key Stage 1 is level 2. This is broken down into A, B and C. Children achieving 2A are working at the top end of the expected level, 2B in the middle and 2C in the early stages of the level. Some more able children go on to achieve level 3, which is not graded. Less able children are awarded level 1 or a W (working towards level 1). The child's chronological age is not taken into account when awarding levels and it should be remembered that some children are still six when they take the tests.

How Should I Use the Practice Papers?

The practice papers provided in this revision guide are similar to the ones your child will take in the actual test. There are two oral tests and two written tests. As with the National Tests, it is not necessary for your child to complete a test in one session and they may have a break while working on the paper. Should your child need help with reading the questions, you can give it. Practical equipment should be offered as support if required – remember the idea is to develop confidence and not to worry your child unnecessarily.

On completion of the practice paper, it is helpful to mark it together, so that you are able to identify any problem areas and work on them. Answers to the practice questions are provided at the back of the book and from the number of marks gained you will have a rough idea of your child's level.

If your child continues to struggle with a subject you should discuss this with their teacher, who may be able to suggest an alternative way of helping your child.

Practice Papers

Oral Test 1

At Key Stage 1, the children will be asked some oral questions before they begin the written test.

Read the following questions to your child. They should write their answers in the boxes on the opposite page.

1. What is double 4? Write your answer in box 1.

2. Look at box 2. Mouse is going to the seaside on Tuesday. What will the date be? Write your answer in box 2.

3. It will take half an hour to get to the sea side. How many minutes is this? Write your answer in box 3.

4. Look at the triangles in box 4. Put a tick by the triangle that has a right angle.

5. Which number comes next in this sequence?
   6, 8, 10, 12, ?

   Write your answer in box 5.

6. Ten minus two leaves …? Write your answer in box 6.

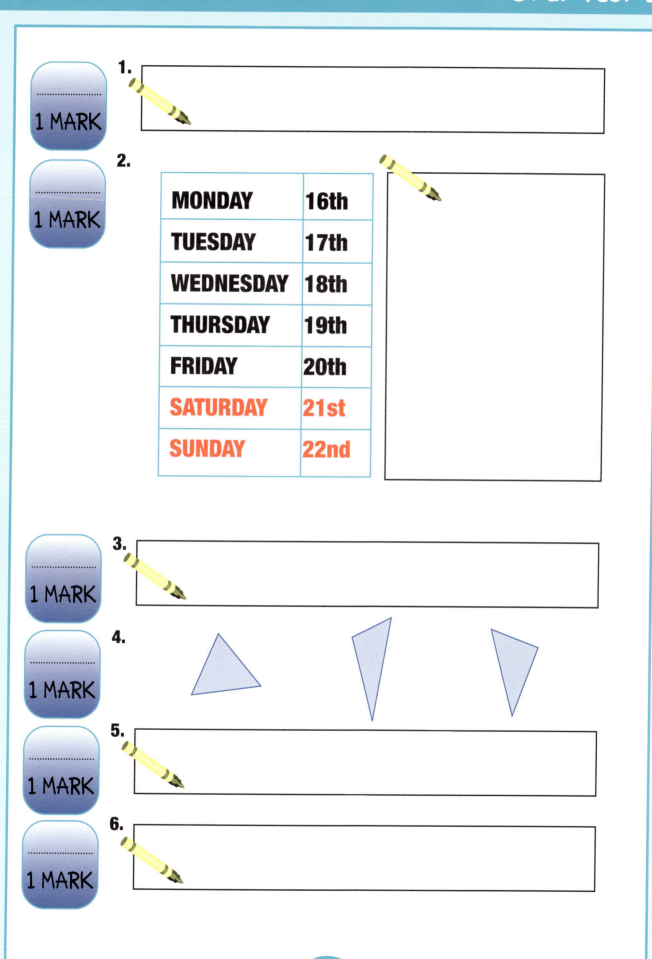

Practice Papers

Test 1

Question Booklet

Name ....

Score ....

Test 1

Instructions

You may read the following questions to your child, but you may not read out the figures or numerals (you cannot say 'thirty' when the numeral 30 is given in the text. Instead you should point to the numeral and say 'this number').

The first question is a practice question. You should use this question to make sure your child understands what they have to do before proceeding with the rest of the test.

If your child wants to, they may write on the question paper to help them work out the answers.

There is no time limit for each question.

PRACTICE QUESTION

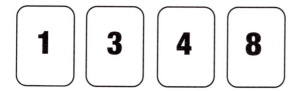

Use two of the cards to make a number **less** than 20. Write your answer in the boxes below.

Practice Papers

1 MARK

1. Use two of the cards on page 43 to make a number **more** than 40. Write your answers in the boxes below.

☐ ☐

2 MARKS

2. Complete this number line:

| 15 | 17 | 19 | ☐ | 23 | 25 | 27 | ☐ |

1 MARK

3. What is the third number in the sequence above?

☐

4. Mouse has used half of his shells to decorate his sandcastles. How many shells has he got left?

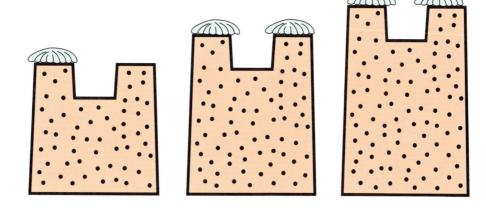

5. Draw an arrow to show which shell is missing from Mouse's pattern.

Practice Papers

4 MARK

6. Match each shape to its name. One has been done for you.

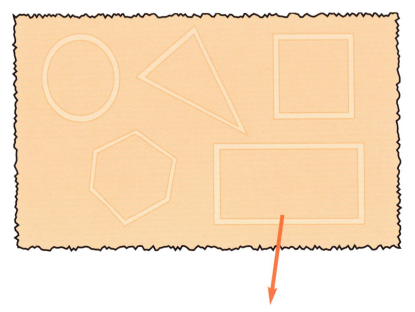

circle   triangle   square   rectangle   hexagon

1 MARK

7. Mouse goes to buy an ice cream at half past eleven. Draw a circle around the watch with the correct time.

8. Mouse buys two ice creams for 25 pence each.

How could he pay using one coin?

9. How could he pay using 3 coins?

Practice Papers

1 MARK

10. Mouse buys two ice creams. Each ice cream has 15 chocolate sprinkles on top. How many chocolate sprinkles are used altogether?

1 MARK

11. How long is the largest ice cream? Use a ruler to measure it.

…… cm

48

Test 1

1 MARK

12. Look at the graph below. How many crabs did Mouse find?

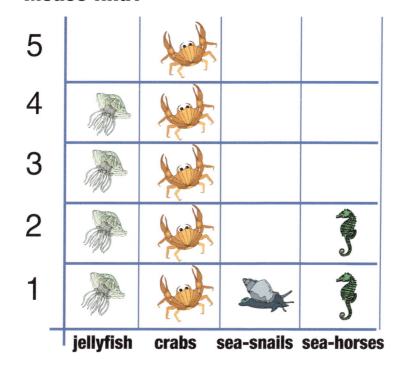

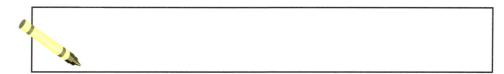

1 MARK

13. What creature did Mouse find 4 of?

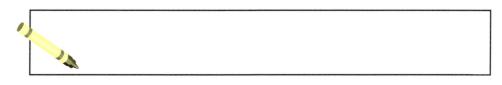

1 MARK

14. 42 to the nearest 10 is 40
78 to the nearest 10 is

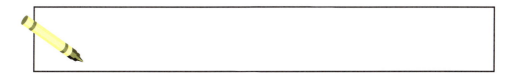

Practice Papers

1 MARK

15. Look at Mouse's bucket. How much seawater has he collected?

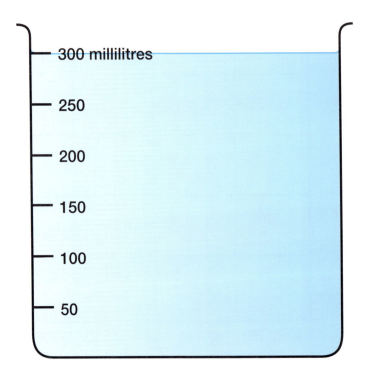

.... millilitres

1 MARK

16. If he pours 200 millilitres into his moat, how much water will be left in the bucket?

.... millilitres

Test 1

1 MARK

17. Choose one of the signs to make this sum correct.

7 ☐ 3 = 4

1 MARK

18.

Put the numbers on the sandcastles in order, from the smallest to the largest.

smallest   largest

51

Practice Papers

1 MARK

19. Draw a line of symmetry through the starfish. You may use a ruler.

1 MARK

20. Seventeen add three equals

Test 1

1 MARK

21.

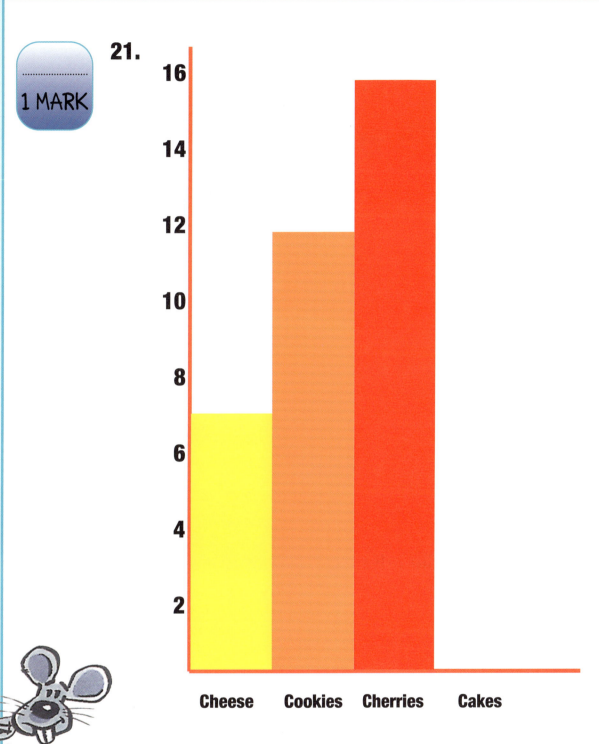

This bar graph shows what Mouse and his friends ate for lunch. They also ate 8 small cakes. Show this on the graph.

1 MARK

22.   4 x 5 = 10 x

Practice Papers

 1 MARK

23. Use 2 of the numbers to make 400.

200   6   75   8   150   2

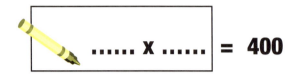
…… x …… = 400

 1 MARK

24. Mouse hired a deck chair at 10 o'clock for 4 hours. What time must he take the chair back?

…… o'clock

 2 MARKS

25. Fill in the missing signs in these questions.

+   −   x   ÷

a) 45 …… 15 = 30

b) 71 …… 23 = 94

c) 67 …… 67 = 0

Test 1

1 MARK

26. Mouse's sandcastle was 50 cm high. His brother's was 35 cm high. How much taller was Mouse's castle?

 cm

1 MARK

27. Mouse has 35 raisins. He shares them between his 5 friends. How many raisins does each mouse get?

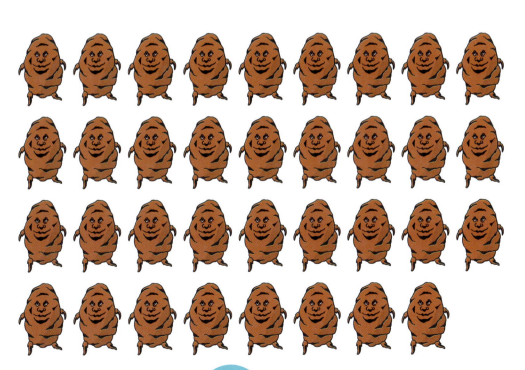

55

Practice Papers

1 MARK

28. 8 ÷ [......] = 4

1 MARK

29. Mouse's crab can walk 50 cm in one minute. If it walks for 5 minutes, how far will it have travelled?

56

1 MARK

30. Mouse has built 20 sandcastles. The sea knocks down a quarter of them. How many sandcastles are left?

Show your working out.

Practice Papers

Oral Test 2

At Key Stage 1, the children will be asked some oral questions before they begin the written test.

Read the following questions to your child. They should write their answers in the boxes on the opposite page.

1. What is 3 add 3? Write your answer in box 1.

2. A hen lays 1 egg a day for 2 weeks. How many eggs does she lay altogether? Write your answer in box 2.

3. Look at the different shapes. How many circular faces does a cylinder have? Write your answer in box 3.

4. Look at the coins. How much do they add up to?

5. There are 2 stables with 4 horses in each. How many horses are there? Write your answer in box 5.

6. Mouse shares a whole biscuit between four friends. How much will they get each? Put a tick next to the right answer.

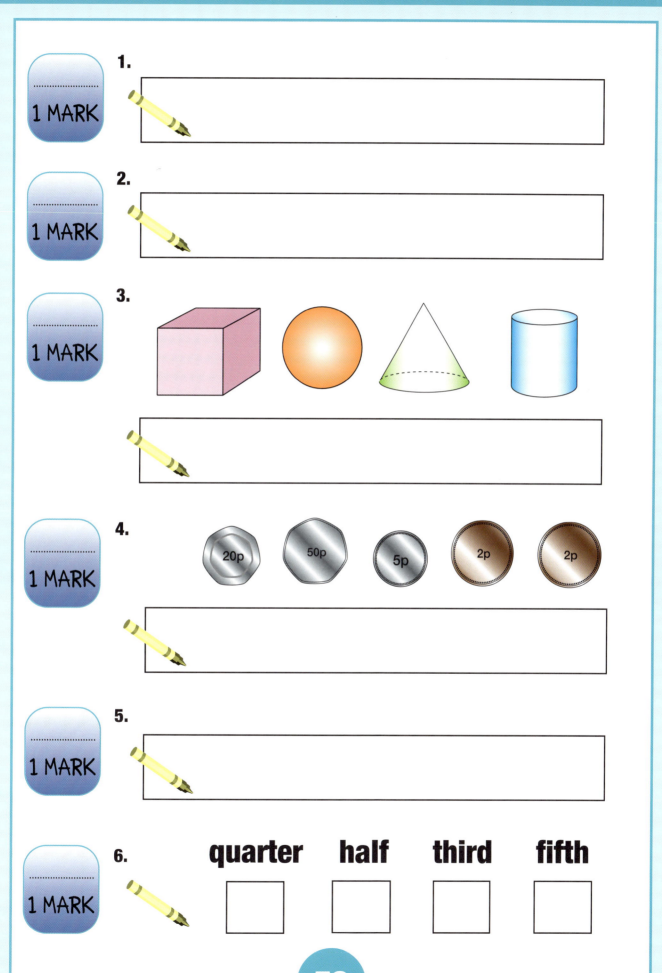

Practice Papers

Test 2

Question Booklet

Name ....

Score ....

Test 2

Instructions

You may read the following questions to your child, but you may not read out the figures or numerals (you cannot say 'thirty' when the numeral 30 is given in the text. Instead you should point to the numeral and say 'this number').

The first question is a practice question. You should use this question to make sure your child understands what they have to do before proceeding with the rest of the test.

If your child wants to, they may write on the question paper to help them work out the answers.

There is no time limit for each question.

PRACTICE QUESTION:

Put a circle round the largest of these numbers

27   72   81   86   42

Practice Papers

1 MARK

1. Put these numbers in order from the largest to the smallest.

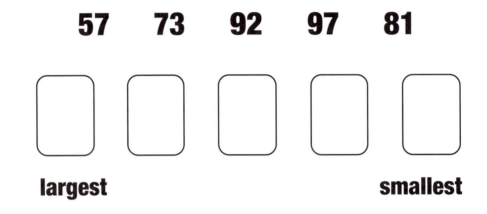

largest   smallest

1 MARK

2. Complete this number sentence:

Ten take away four equals ☐

62

Test 2

3. Circle the 2D shape that has 7 straight edges.

4. Fill in the missing number on the grid.

| 3 | 6 | 9 | 12 | | 18 |

Practice Papers

1 MARK

5. The numbers below the pigs show how many piglets each pig has got.

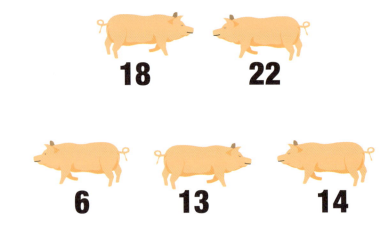

Put a circle around the pig which has an odd number of piglets.

1 MARK

6. A new collar for the sheep dog costs £1.20. It costs an extra 50p for the name to be written on the collar. What is the total cost?

Test 2

7. What number is 4 less than 16?

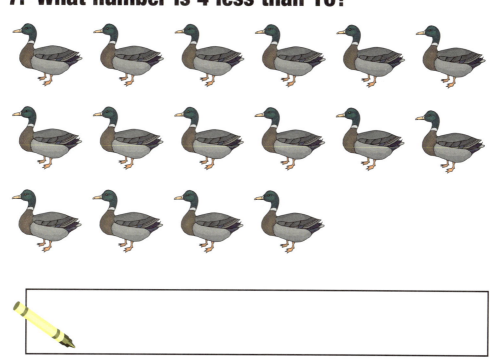

8. What would be the 10th number in this sequence?

2, 4, 6, 8, 10, 12

9. 1 pig eats eat 3 bags of food a day. How many bags of food would it take to feed 12 pigs for 1 day?

Practice Papers

1 MARK

10. Which 3D shape should the mouse use for a new wheel for his tractor? Circle the answer.

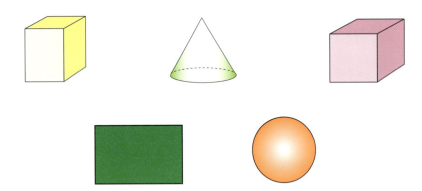

1 MARK

11. Complete this question:

12 + 9 =

1 MARK

12. Draw the lines to show how to share this pie equally between 4 farmers.

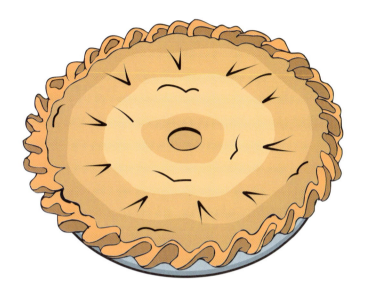

3 MARKS

13. Draw a line to link the numbers on the top row to the nearest 10. One has been done for you:

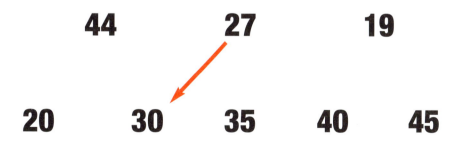

Practice Papers

14. 5 ducks live on the farm. Each duck lays 6 eggs. How many eggs are laid altogether?

This graph shows how many eggs the chickens laid over one week.

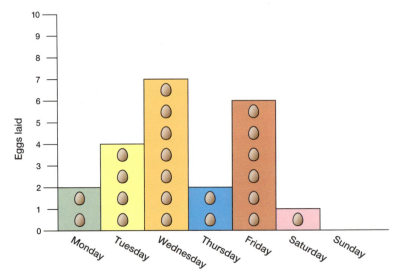

15. How many eggs were laid on Tuesday?

16. How many more eggs were laid on Wednesday than Thursday?

17. Ten eggs were laid on Sunday. Show this on the graph.

18. Put an 'x' on the sheep standing next to the tree.

19. Put an 'x' on the chicken in front of the fence.

20. Put an 'x' on the cow behind the fence.

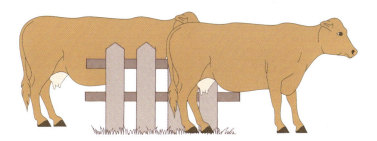

21. Complete this question:

19 − ☐ = 12

Practice Papers

1 MARK

22. Measure the horses' tails using a ruler. Which horse has the longest tail, A or B? Put a tick next to the correct answer.

A.

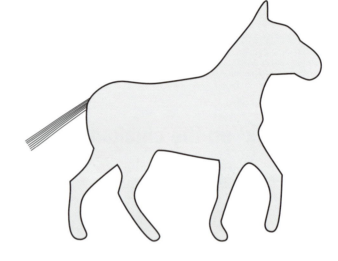

B.

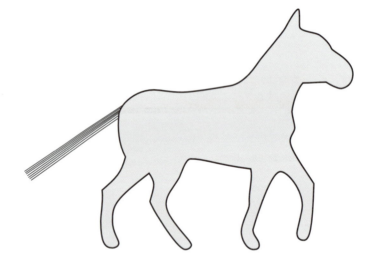

1 MARK

23. Fill in the missing number in this sequence:

20   40   ☐   160   320

Test 2

24. How much does the calf weigh?

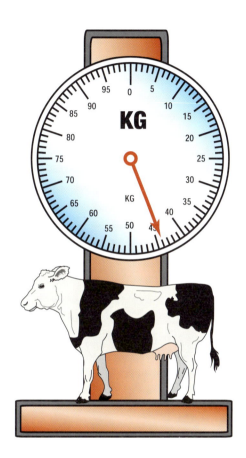

 kg

25. Complete this question.

15 + 4 + 3 = ☐

Practice Papers

1 MARK

26. Estimate the length of the pig's tail. You can't use a ruler, so do a 'thought-about' guess.

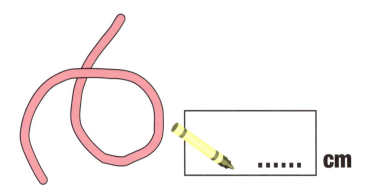

1 MARK

27. Draw a rectangle that measures 4 spots wide and 6 spots long.

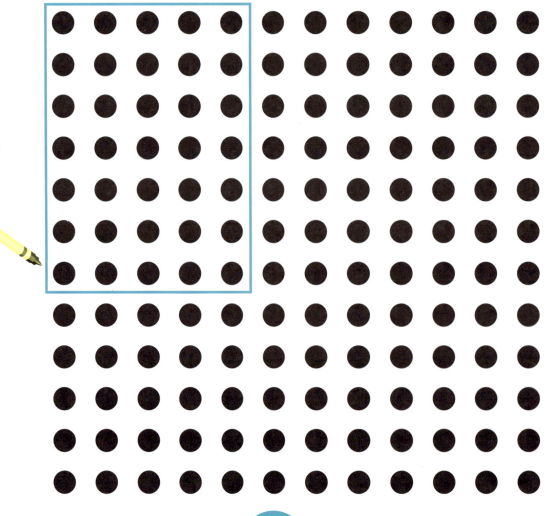

72

28. Mouse sees some apples for sale in a farm shop.

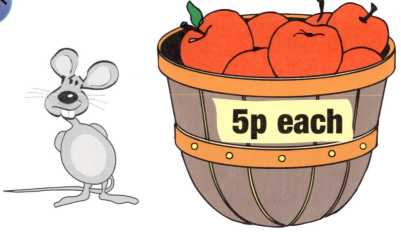

This is how much money Mouse has:

2p   2p   1p   5p   10p   2p

How many apples can Mouse buy? (Show your working out.)

Practice Papers

1 MARK

29.

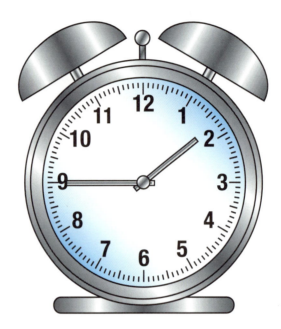

The farmer started milking at this time. She finished milking 45 minutes later. Show the time on the clock when she finished milking.

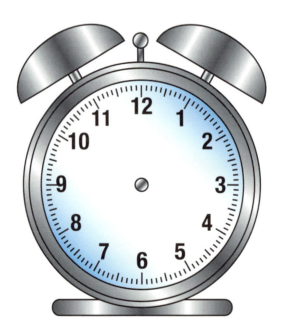

2 MARKS

30. Use these number cards to make the biggest 3-digit number.

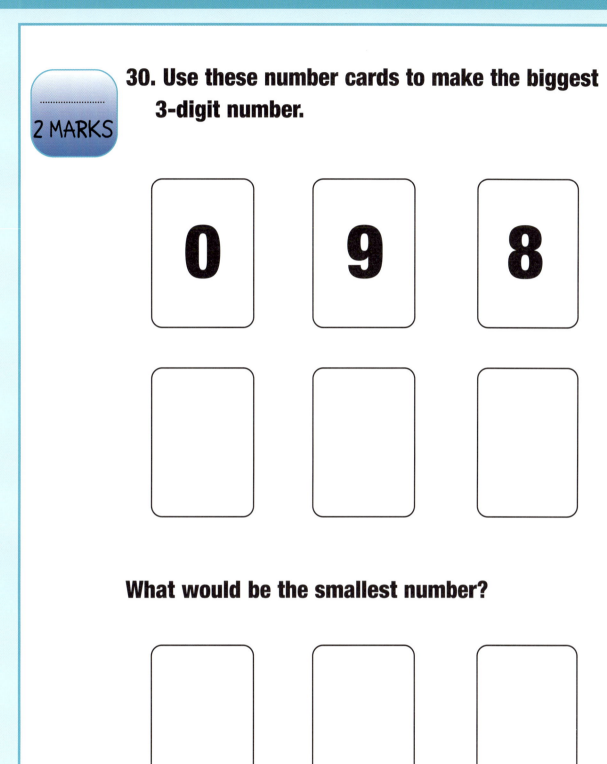

What would be the smallest number?

75

Practice Papers

Answers to Oral Test 1 and Test 1

Oral Test 1

One mark should be given for each correct answer.

1. 8
2. 17th
3. 30 (minutes)
4. The last triangle is the right-angle triangle
5. 14
6. 8

Test 1

When you mark your child's paper, it is helpful if you do this with them, talking through the questions and their workings.

Add up your child's score out of the maximum of 42 marks (for Oral Test 1 and Test 1). Once you have marked all the questions, see the bottom of page 79 to determine what level they may be working to.

Practice question: 13, 14, or 18

76

Answers: Test 1

1. 41, 43, 48, 81, 83, or 84
2. 21, 29
3. 19
4. 6
5. cone
6. check paper
7. 11:30
8. 50p
9. 20p, 20p, 10p
10. 30
11. 10 cm
12. 5 (crabs)
13. jellyfish
14. 80
15. 300 millilitres
16. 100 millilitres
17. –
18. 13, 25, 42, 64, 79
19. check paper
20. twenty/20
21. check paper - bar should come up to no. 8
22. 4 x 5 = 10 x 2
23. 200 x 2
24. 2 o'clock
25. a) 45 – 15 = 30; b) 71 + 23 = 94; c) 67 – 67 = 0
26. 15 cm
27. 7 raisins each
28. 8 ÷ 2 = 4
29. 250 cm
30. 15 sand castles are left. Children's workings to show that they have attempted to divide 20 into 4 groups to find out what a quarter is, then to have counted the remainder.

Practice Papers

Answers to Oral Test 2 and Test 2

Oral Test 2

One mark should be given for each correct answer.

1. 6
2. 14
3. 2
4. 79p
5. 8
6. quarter

Test 2

When you mark your child's paper, it is helpful if you do this with them, talking through the questions and their workings.

Add up your child's score out of the maximum of 39 marks (for Oral Test 2 and Test 2). Once you have marked all the questions, see the bottom of page 79 to determine what level they may be working to.

Practice question: 86

1. 97, 92, 81, 73, 57
2. 6
3. check that the shape has 7 straight edges
4. 15
5. 13
6. £1.70
7. 12

Answers: Test 2

8. 20
9. 36
10. sphere
11. 21
12. check that the cake has been divided into quarters
13. 44 – 40, 27 – 30, 19 – 20
14. 30 eggs
15. 4
16. 5
17. check on the graph that your child has drawn a line level with the 10
18. check paper
19. check paper
20. check paper
21. 7
22. B
23. 80
24. 44 kg
25. 22
26. answers between 7 cm and 13 cm
27. check paper
28. 4 apples. Working out might show children have attempted to group the coins into sums of 5p.
29. hands to have been drawn indicating 2.30 pm. Check that the hour hand is shorter than the minute hand, and that it is between numbers 2 and 3 on the clock face. The minute hand should be longer and pointing directly at the 6.
30. 980 = largest number   089 = smallest number

Levels: Key Stage One

The following bands suggest the level at which your child is probably working:

Number of questions correct: 5–7:   Level 1
8–13:   Level 2C
14–18: Level 2B
19–24: Level 2A
25–36: Level 3

By the end of Year 2 it expected that most children will be working at level 2B or 2A

Practice Papers

Answers to Revision Guide Questions

Page 6
1. 61
2. 58
3. 5
4. 5

Page 7
2. 14
   49
   70
3. 85

Page 9
1. Horizontally the numbers go along in 1s and vertically in 10s. Each square has one number in it.
2. 10, 20, 30, 40, 50; etc
3. 2, 4, 6, 8, 10, 12, etc

Page 10
1. 0 + 10
   1 + 9
   2 + 8
   3 + 7
   4 + 6
   5 + 5
   6 + 4
   7 + 3
   8 + 2
   9 + 1
   10 + 0

Page 12
Activities
1. 7
2. 2
3. 9

Questions
1. 2
2. 8
3. 12 – 8 & open ended
4. Two
5. Four

Page 14
Question
1. 2; 8; 6; 12

Page 15
Questions
1. 2; 8; 4; 6
2. 1; 4; 2; 3

Activities
1. 5
2. 8

Page 16
1. 2nd, 3rd and 4th pictures
2. 2
3. 8

Page 17
1. 1st and 3rd jar

Page 19
Questions
1. 9
2. 12
3. 50

Activities
1. 15
2. 18
3. 70
4. 6
5. 20
6. 40

Page 21
Question
1. 3 x 2; 2 x 5; 4 x 5; 2 x 10

Page 22
1. x; –; +; ÷
2. 12
3. 8
4. 10
5. 10

Page 23
Question
Line 1: 9, 13, 15
Line 2: 18, 14, 8, 4
Line 3: 13, 19, 22

Activities
1.
   3 4 5 5 3 4 4 5 3

2.

③
④ ⑤
② ⑥ ①

Page 24
1. Shampoo: 6.2 cm
   Soap: 4.1 cm
   Toothbrush: 5.0 cm
   Razor: 5.0 cm
2. Shampoo
3. Soap

Page 26
1. 150 g
2. 100 g
3. 50 g
4. There are 1000 grams in a kilogram

Page 27
Question
Blue: 3 cm
Red: 2.5 cm - accept 2 cm or 3 cm
Green: 1 cm
Yellow: 2 cm
Orange: 1 cm

Page 31
2. The top right one (with the mouse looking sideways)

Page 32
Activity
Check the child's answer as they say it

Page 35
Questions
1. 50p and 1p
2. most: £2, 20p, 5p
   least: 1p, 1p, 1p
3. Harriet spent 70p, she got 30p change. One way is 1 x 20p and 1 x 10p, there are many other ways.

Activities
1. Harriet has £2.43
2. Tom has £2.32
3. Harriet

Page 37
Questions
1. 4
2. August and November
3. None
4. April
5. Two